I0163078

WHO
ARE
You?

MOUNTAIN OF FIRE AND MIRACLES MINISTRIES

DR. D. K. OLUKOYA

Who are you?

Dr Daniel Olukoya

Who are you?
©2010.Dr Daniel Olukoya

A publication of
MOUNTAIN OF FIRE AND MIRACLES MINISTRIES
13, Olasimbo Street, off Olumo Road, Onike,
P. O. Box 2990, Sabo, Yaba, Lagos, Nigeria.

ISBN: **978-0692490631**

For further information or permission contact:
Email: pasteurdanielolukoya_french@yahoo.fr
           mfmhqworldwide@mountainoffire.org

Or visit our website: www.mountainoffire.org
http://mfmbiligualbooks4evangelism.blogspot.com/

Mathew 16:13-18: "When Jesus came into the coasts of Caesarea Philippi, he asked his disciples, saying: "*Whom do men say that I the Son of man am?*" And they said" "*Some say that Thou art John the Baptist: some, Elias; and others, Jeremias, or one of the prophets*". He saith unto them: "*But whom say ye that I am?*" And Simon Peter answered and said: "*Thou art the Christ, the Son of the living God*". And Jesus answered and said unto him: "*Blessed art thou, Simon Barjona: for flesh and blood hath not revealed it unto thee, but my Father which is in heaven. And I say also unto thee, That thou art Peter, and upon this rock I will build my church; and the gates of hell shall not prevail against it*".

Beloved, this is a day to identify the deepest root of problems and failure. John 1:19-23: "*And this is the record of John, when the Jews sent priests and Levites from Jerusalem to ask him: "Who art thou?" And he confessed, and denied not; but confessed: "I am not the Christ". And they asked him: "What then? Art thou Elias?" And he saith: "I am not". "Art thou that prophet?" And he answered: "No". Then said they unto him: "Who art thou? That we may give an answer to them that sent us. What sayest thou of thyself?" He said: "I am the voice of one crying in the wilderness: "Make straight the way of the Lord, as said the prophet Esaias".*

The difference between the rich and the poor is information. One has the information that will advance him in life and the other does not have it. Sometimes, the difference between the great and the small is knowledge. There is a saying that: "A man's mountain is his ignorance". Men have made many outstanding discoveries; the fellow who invented the telephone was mocked, because it looked like a toy but today, it has become an indispensable tool in everyday life. When the young men who invented the aeroplane started it in the back of their yard, people laughed them to scorn. When the fellow who invented the motor car was testing it around, people told him to keep it aside and buy a horse, like every other person; he persisted and succeeded, Christopher Columbus discovered America; Mungo Park discovered River Niger and their names are inscribed in gold today, in history. There are great discoveries, but the greatest discovery that anyone could ever make, is Self-discovery. There is no greater discovery than that. It is possible for a person to be born again, Spirit-filled, sanctified, and could be a Pastor or Evangelist, without knowing who he or she is. That is why this question is coming out to you today: WHO ARE YOU? It is a very important question; it is like asking for your identity card. Ignorance about who you are could put you in untold hardship.

The lesson on identity is very important. Jacob learnt this lesson; he saw that by his identity, he was not in his place of destiny. He got the blessings meant for his brother Esau; got his identity through fowl means but he later discovered that, that did not help him. He had to hold tight to the Angel of the Lord and his identity was changed. He was given a new name, before he could actually enjoy any blessing. One of Satan's most effective devices is to get Christians, to be completely ignorant of their true identity. The devil is an expert at doing this; he tried it on Jesus, so he will do it to any Christian. The devil thought he could confuse Jesus, by saying: *"If Thou be the Son of God, command these stones to become bread"* What was the devil trying to do? It was to make Jesus doubt His identity. It means if Jesus did not know Who He is, the devil would have gotten away with his trick. That did not discourage the devil; he tried again, by saying: *"If Thou be the Son of God, cast yourself down; because it is written that the angels will bear you in their arms"*. Again, Jesus defeated him, but that did not stop the devil from trying again at the Cross; he spoke through the people who mocked Jesus, telling Him to come down from the Cross, if He was truly the Son of God. The devil is an expert at speaking to Christians; he would want to convince them, that as children of God, they are not supposed to suffer so, their suffering, means that God is not with them, or that He is partial or wicked. The devil would ask if your God is asleep. Beloved, why are you entertaining evil thoughts? I am asking once more: "Who are you? Some people, when they pray, call themselves all kinds of names; they will say they are unworthy servants, miserable sinners, unfit, unworthy, bad, etc Some of them think that by so doing, they are being humble; all they are doing, is to appropriate upon themselves, satanic identity card. It actually shows that they do not know who they are. The devil will always try to whisper dirty things into the ears of the believer. Whilst the believer is busy thinking about it, he will turn round and accuse the person and even report him or her to God. The person will be found guilty on many grounds and will be discouraged. The prodigal son did a lot of terrible things. He was rotten and bad. The Bible records that he got to a stage in his life, when he came to his senses and realised that he needed a change in his situation. His head became 'correct' and he realised the son of whom he was; a son and not a slave; he decided that he would arise and go to his father and he did. The devil will whip people forward and backwards, if they do not know who they are.

You must know who you are. Let the life of Jesus, from His birth to His death on the Cross, be an example to you. Jesus was always talking about whom and what He is, what His mission in life is. He said He is the Living Water, the Bread of Life, the Son of God, the Way, the Truth and the Life. Who are you? I am not asking what your name is; at this level, your name is not important. You could put a donkey somewhere and call it a horse; dress it like a horse, it will not mind.

When the time comes and you ask it to run, it is then that everybody will know that even though its name is Mr. Horse, it is a donkey and not a horse. Who are you? What is your spiritual ability? If you do not know the answers to these questions, you will be like those that were praying for the release of Peter from prison, but did not expect to see him at the door. The day you realise who you are, that day, you would have won a great battle. Maybe God is telling you to pray for some people or preach to them and you are giving excuses and feeling unworthy; it is very dangerous. This feeling of unworthiness has made many Christians to become targets for the devil. When you know who you are, and you keep confessing it, things begin to happen.

The soldiers that were sent to capture Elijah asked him to come down from the mountain and he said if he really was a man of God, fire should come down and it did. All the witches and wizards in this environment and in the world at large cannot overcome me. Can you say that of yourself, or are you afraid of them? Who are you? Many people do not know who they are, when the devil comes; they do not know which answer to give to him. People asked John who he was; thank God he knew who he was and he told them that he was the 'voice, crying in the wilderness'.

Many years ago, a man prophesied a 'strange' prophecy. He was a fervent and diligent Christian. He was always the first to get to the church on service days; he was very zealous for the Lord. He was known to be a prophet. On that day, he prophesied that in a few years from then, men would walk on the moon; people found it funny and told the Pastor that he should be careful, who he allows to prophesy in the church; that he was confusing people with strange sayings. A prophet does not argue; he believed he was speaking the mind of God. Seven years after the man died, some astronauts went to the Moon and the whole world heard it. The man knew who he was. Do you know who you are?

Some people vaunt themselves in their occultist exploits; they claim to be powerful witches and wizards. What good is in doing evil? What good is in eating up your children? Is there any sense in rendering your children useless, and hindering their progress, to the extent that they cannot stand on their own and cannot help you in old age? It does not make sense at all. Beloved, how many children of witches have you seen, obtaining scholarship to study abroad or become great in life? They do not allow them, except that child gives his or her life to the Lord Jesus Christ and is delivered completely. If you have any evil spirit, or you belong to any evil or occultist group, you had better come out of it. It means you are in a group of limitation; get out of it and discover your identity. It has been said, that the greatest enemy of Man, is himself; not the devil or anybody else. I had a White friend, who would wake up in the morning, go to a mirror to see himself and ask his image how it is, and how the day would be.

What is the most terrible form of Man's ignorance? It is ignorance of oneself; not knowing what one is. If you do not know who you are, you are in a dangerous position. That is why some people worship animals and feed them with the food that people should eat, whilst they are dying of hunger. When a woman was in the world, she used to get prostitution business for her friends, who would pay her a certain percentage of what they got from their clients. She would stand by and collect her money up-front. One evening, she got a man for her friend and they went into a hotel room. She was outside, parading. Suddenly, she heard her friend scream from inside the room. It persisted and she had to peep through the key-hole. She saw her friend naked but did not see the man. She then noticed that there was a snake curling round the friend. She wanted to scream or run away, but she was too scared. She felt the man could harm her, so she kept calm. Eventually, they came out and she was expecting the friend to recount her ordeal to her, but she did not. Rather, she praised the man as being nice. That friend knew what she was, but this woman, did not.

A woman went to an office to advertise artificial hair to another lady. She left a sample and promised to go back there. The client waited for some weeks but the seller did not come. She then decided to get it fixed on her head. Right from that moment, she started to dream of her former boyfriends, hear strange voices that would order her to do strange things. She would see herself combing her hair in the dream and instead of seeing strands of hair fall off, she saw tiny fishes and cray-fish, drop from her head. She then understood that there was a problem. She tried to trace the woman, by the address that the she left. On getting there, the client discovered that it was a cemetery. This is a real life experience; that is why in MFM, we tell people to avoid certain things. People think we are too conservative or restrictive; but, is it not better for you to be avoid these artificial things that will get you into trouble, than to look artificially beautiful and be in spiritual bondage? The woman that came to advertise the attachment knew what she was doing; but the one who took it and fixed it on her head, is the one that was ignorant. She did not know who she was spiritually. This is a deep truth; many people in the world do not know who they are.

Another deadly disease is self-hatred; some people hate themselves with perfect hatred and this leads to jealousy, fear, pride, deception, wickedness, anger, lesbianism, homosexuality, masturbation, sodomy, inordinate affection, and all kinds of sexual confusion and perversion. A person with self-hatred sees every other person, by the perception that he or she has of himself or herself. If a man hates himself so much, as to pump cocaine or other hard drugs into his blood-stream, there is no way that the person would treat other people in a better way. If a woman hates herself so much, as to prostitute, there is no way she would treat other people in a better way. The trouble is that people judge others the way they judge themselves. They regard others the way they value themselves. Until you discover who you are, you cannot give yourself unselfishly to another person. That is why many marriages are in trouble today. If Mr. Zero marries Miss Zero, they become Mr. & Mrs. Zero that is, they are nobody; meaning that there is no marriage. If Mr. Chronic Selfishness marries Miss Acute Selfishness, they become Selfishness2 ; meaning there is no marriage. Many people get into wrong marriages, because they have not discovered who they are. One day, I saw a young man, cuddling an old woman. I felt very embarrassed and I moved close and asked him to give his mother, breathing space. The woman answered me sharply, saying she begged my pardon, that the young man was her husband and not her son. Later, I had the opportunity of seeing the young man alone and I asked him why he was in that kind of relationship.

He said it paid off, because the woman was rich and he did not have to work. He had all that he needed. He was about twenty one years old, while the woman was about sixty.

That young man did not know who he was. There are many people like that. What we are saying in essence, is that 99% of married people, never really know themselves. When two people who do not know themselves get married, there will be confusion and their children too, will be confused. There are many people like that, who really never discover themselves. Some women are looking out for a husband that would pet them and take them to picnics every week-end, whereas, the kind of husband they need, is the one that will kick them here and there, and that will move them to pray hard and will make them candidates of heaven. The one that they wanted would have pampered them and they would not have remembered God.

Symptoms of not Knowing Oneself

1. *Complete ignorance of one's divine destiny*: When a person does not know why God created him or her, and put him or her, where he or she is. If you are forty or fifty years old and you do not yet know why you are in this world, you have to pray seriously today; time is running out on the human race. Now is the time to discover who you are and why God brought you to the world.

2. *When a person possesses a deep sense of self-hatred, self-rejection, self-condemnation:* This is the feeling of being unwanted, being unneeded, unloved, withdrawal and isolation, lack of initiative, lack of motivation etc. Some men cannot take personal decisions; they have to consult their mother before they can do anything. Some people cannot start anything until someone motivates them.

Some students cannot study on their own; it is when the examination is approaching that they will start running here and there, doing crash programmes, cramming things, taking drugs to stay awake, etc and this is what leads to examination mal-practices. The feelings of inadequacy, hopelessness, weakness, are all evidence that the person has not discovered himself. Negative complaints, jealousy, unforgiveness, resentment, intolerance, suspicion, regular depression, greed, over-sensitivity. All these are signs that a person has not discovered himself and if a person does not discover himself, his potentials will be completely paralysed.

What I am saying, beloved, is very deep; many people have been buried and must come to the surface. If a person has been buried, in the ground or in the bottom of the river, he or she cannot breathe; therefore, has to come to the surface.

Take this prayer point with holy madness:

- *I refuse to be buried alive in the Name of Jesus*.

There are many people, who are dead, but are still living. Many died long ago but in God's arithmetic, they never even existed on earth, some are still alive, but by God's arithmetic, they are non-existent. God created each of us for a particular purpose and if you do not fulfill that purpose, it is as if you never showed up on earth; you are present, but absent. You arrived on earth, but did not show up.

Beloved, the truth of the matter, is that many people are what their parents, want them to become, not what the Almighty wants them to be. Some are what their environment made them to become. Some are what people say they should become, some are what they themselves decided to become. Only a few people are really what God wants them to become. It means most people never really showed up on earth. Beloved, if you want to be very effective, you must discover who you are.

One day, a sister prayed fervently that God should show her who she is. That night, she had a dream, where she saw herself in the company of her friends. An angel told her that one of the friends was a cow, the other, a dog and she was a leaf. She rejoiced, saying that she was not an animal. She did not realise that her being a leaf, meant being without substance, consumable to others. Some years later, she became a psychiatric patient; household wickedness had dealt with her. It is a pity to note that many people are in this kind of situation; household wickedness would recreate their destiny; they resize the destiny of people and make them useless to themselves and to the society. What many people are carrying about and rejoicing is not God's original plan for their life.

Take these prayer points:

- *I reject every demonic recreation of my destiny, in the Name of Jesus.*
- *I will reach my goal whether the devil likes it or not, in the Name of Jesus.*
Are you a preacher or pastor, because you want to be one? Or you are, because that is what God wants you to be? One day, there was an ordination service and the Choir was singing. The Pastor-in-charge came out to address the would-be Pastors: he said some

of them were there because they opted for it as a profession, on their own, that is, they called themselves. Some were there, because the church called them, some were there, because God called them, some were there because the devil called them. He said each of them should know who called him and why. He went on to say that they would all be ordained, but when they get out on the field, their work will show who called them and for what purpose. Are you a business man because you like it or because God wants you to be one? Are you a musician or banker, or lawyer, or doctor because you or your parents want you to be one? Or because God called you to be one? Are you still intact? Are you still God's original design? Or you have been unconsciously altered by the enemies of your destiny? Are you where you are because it is your place of destiny? It is important to discover this. When God created Man, He gave him several assignments.

The first thing that God gave to Man, is an image; the Bible says God made Man in His own image; since God is not a failure, Man should not be a failure. What is your original personal image? If you do not have yourself, you do not have anything. This is why human opinion about me, does not give me, nor remove any value from me. When you discover yourself, you will be free from the effect of the opinion of other people; you will not get swollen or deflated by what people say about you. You will not be bothered by their comments on your relationship with God. You will not be worn out by the comments of people, on your decision to dress modestly, when you know who you are.

Jesus asked the disciples, who men say He is and then, who they themselves say He is. For Him to have asked the question, He knew the answer; that is why, when Peter said He is the Son of God and Saviour of the world, shown in the flesh, Jesus affirmed that the Spirit of God was in Peter, to have answered correctly. Whatever you think about someone who knows who he is does not matter. The only One who knows who you are is God, Who made you. If you ask Him, He will tell you who you are. The closer you get to God, the more you know about yourself. You must discover, or rediscover yourself. The moment you believe you are nobody, you are off the track and the devil will make you believe all kinds of lies about yourself. You need to get back in touch with who you are. The moment you discover yourself, your value comes back; your worth comes back. No opinion can devalue it. It is not what you have that makes you valuable, but what you are as a person.

The Yoruba have an adage that says: "It is not the big size of your dress that makes you a big man" That is, you could be a mean person, putting on big regalia; that does not make you big. The collar on the neck of a Pastor is not what makes him a pastor. It is just a part of the uniform that shows him as pastor. The palace does not make you a king. It is just a kind of accommodation; it is the King that turns that building into a palace. The Bible calls us 'Royal Priesthood' When you discover who you are, things will not give you value anymore; but things will become valuable because you possess them. I hope you understand what I am saying. When the President of a foreign country went to an African country, he was welcomed and traditional attire was put on him. That did not turn him into an African; it did not remove nor add any value to him.

Rather, the attire could be said to have become a presidential garment, because it was worn by a President; he was the one that gave the attire value. Very soon, people would want to put on that kind of attire and it will be in vogue; they might even name the style after the President. So if you know what you are doing, you will give value to it and will not allow circumstances and things around you to control you. What I am saying in essence, is that you should place value on yourself. Do not deceive yourself nor allow others to deceive you.

One of the greatest forms of deception I have come across, is when an intending couple, go about borrowing things for their wedding. Some borrow cars and by the following day, after they must have returned the car, they will be running after commuter buses as usual. Some borrow money and after the wedding, they will be running away from creditors. It is deception of the highest order; that is why you should take this prayer point:

- *Every satanic opinion about my life, be shattered to pieces in the Name of Jesus.* The Bible says we are a royal priesthood; a chosen generation; that is why everything about us, should be kingly and royal.

How to discover yourself

1. You must be born again
2. Pray to discover who you are; what God created you to come and do in this world. Know what God had in mind in the beginning, when He created you. If God shows you what He created you to be and to do; you will know if you are doing it or not and you will make moves to change, so that you can be blessed.

3. See yourself, think and talk about yourself the way God does and not the way the devil does.

4. Disconnect yourself from past negative experiences. Paul says: "Forgetting those things that are behind, I look forward..." Some people continue to blame themselves for past mistakes and keep attributing present problems to what they did in their time of ignorance. When God forgives, He forgets; that is why we have to come before Him, in complete and genuine repentance.

5. Do not compare yourself with other people because you are unique. Each person is different from another. The Bible says there is no wisdom in comparing oneself to another.

6. Watch your tongue and especially, what you say about yourself. Do you know that

the words that you speak about yourself and your situation matter a lot? Those things that you playfully say, or that you say in annoyance, even though you did not mean those things, matter.

7. Have wise friends; those who will make your life better. Anyone that advises you to marry an unbeliever because you are getting old is not a friend, but a destroyer; even if he or she calls himself a Christian.

8. Walk in holiness, honesty and integrity. The Bible says: "Nothing good shall He withhold from them that walk uprightly.

9. Always think positively; do not engage in negative thoughts. The Bible says: "As a man thinketh in his heart, so is he.

10. Avoid negative and destructive influences. If you notice that the things that someone else is doing, are affecting you negatively, you had better run. If you find out that whenever you move close to

the opposite sex, your body reacts, when the person is not your wife or husband, you had better run. Do not wait until you are captured, before looking for a way of escape from prison.

Today is a day that you must cry to the Lord; talk to Him, ask if you are in the wrong place; perhaps you do not know who you are and what you should be doing. Some people who should not be thinking of marriage yet, are getting married, because they do not know who they are; they do not know their purpose in life; so, they are making mistakes and having problems. Cry unto the Lord today beloved.

We thank God that He can draw straight lines with our crooked lines. Beloved, WHO ARE YOU? You must find that out today. If you are not yet born again, you have never at one time in your life, decided to surrender your life to the Lord Jesus Christ, it means you have not yet started the journey. We thank God that you can still take that decision today; the Lord is with you right there where you are and is ready to save you. All you need do is acknowledge the fact that you are a sinner, and that you cannot approach God in your sinful state. Repent of your sins; confess them to the Lord and ask Him to forgive you and cleanse you from all unrighteousness. Name your sins one by one and renounce them. Make up your mind that you will never go back to them anymore. Take that decision today and your life will never remain the same again.

Invite the Lord Jesus into your life; ask Him to come into your life and become your personal Lord and Saviour. Open the door of your heart and let the Lord come in. Ask Him to take control of your life and all that concerns you.

I congratulate you for taking the decision to become born again. It is the most important decision in life and I pray that it shall be permanent in your life, in the Name of Jesus. I pray that the Lord will uphold you with His right hand of righteousness and will not let you fall. I pray that He will write your name in the Book of Life and you will not allow anything to rub it off in the Name of Jesus. The Bible says you are now a new creature, because you are now in Christ. Draw close to Him and you will see that the Lord is good.

The prayers that I am suggesting below, are meant to make things happen in your life; if you have embarked on a fruitless journey on the wrong path of life, the Holy Spirit will frustrate that journey and turn you to the right path, in the Name of Jesus. Take these prayer points with all the aggression and seriousness that you can gather:

1. Every damage done to my destiny, be repaired by fire, in the Name of Jesus.
2. O Lord, restore me to Your original design for my life, in the Name of Jesus.
3. I reject destiny-demoting names in the Name of Jesus.
4. O Lord, lay Your hands of fire upon my life in the Name of Jesus.
5. O Lord enlarge my coast in the Name of Jesus.
6. I receive explosive breakthrough in the Name of Jesus.
7. O Lord anoint my eyes, ears and legs, to locate my divine purpose.
8. Every power contending with my divine destiny, scatter in the Name of Jesus.

ABOUT D. K. OLUKOYA

Dr. D. K. Olukoya is the General Overseer of the Mountain of Fire and Miracles Ministries and the Battle Cry Ministries. He holds a First Class Honours Degree in Microbiology from the University of Lagos, Nigeria and a Ph.D. in Molecular Genetics from the University of Reading, United Kingdom. As a researcher, he has over eighty scientific publications to his credit. Anointed by God, Dr. Olukoya is a teacher, prophet, evangelist and preacher of the word. His life and that of his wife, Shade and their son, Elijah Toluwani, are living proofs that all power belongs to God.

ABOUT MOUNTAIN OF FIRE AND MIRACLES MINISTRIES

Mountain of Fire and Miracles Ministries, is a ministry devoted to the revival of apostolic signs, Holy Ghost fireworks and the unlimited demonstration of the power of God to deliver to the uttermost. Absolute holiness within and without, as the greatest spiritual insecticide, and a condition for heaven is taught openly. MFM is a do-it-yourself Gospel Ministry, where your hands are trained to wage war and your fingers to fight.

A brief history of Mountain of Fire and Miracles Ministries Incorporated
The Mountain of Fire and Miracles was founded in 1989. The first meeting was held at the home of Dr. D. K Olukoya and had 24 persons in attendance. The Church later moved to No. 60, Old Yaba Road, Lagos, and

then to the present International Headquarters, site on 24th April, 1994. The Mountain of Fire and Miracles Ministries' Headquarters is the largest single Christian congregation in Africa, with attendance of over 200,000 in single meetings. Mountain of Fire and Miracles Ministries is a full gospel ministry devoted to the revival of apostolic signs, Holy Ghost fireworks and the unlimited demonstration of the power of God to deliver to the uttermost. Absolute holiness, within and without, as the greatest spiritual insecticide and a pre-requisite for heaven is taught openly. MFM is a do-it-yourself Gospel ministry, where your hands are trained to wage war and your fingers to do battle.